# WOOD DUCK ADVENTURES

## By F. Eugene Hester

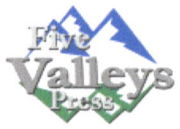

Five Valleys Press
Missoula, Montana 59803
www.FiveValleysPress.com
info@fivevalleyspress.com

International Standard Book Number: 978-0-9835442-7-2

# DEDICATION

This book is dedicated to Jack F. Dermid who provided tremendous encouragement, collaboration and support for this work. His outstanding photography and observations of the intimate details of the nesting process, especially the hatching and exodus from the nests were invaluable. We developed a unique friendship and partnership which has continued for more than half a century.

# CONTENTS

# INTRODUCTION

The perfect partnership is sometimes defined as one in which each person feels they have the better half of the deal. That is what happened back in 1953 when a wildlife researcher and a wildlife photographer started working together. It was the beginning of a relationship in which we had complementary interests and skills of great mutual benefit. The researcher was F. Eugene Hester, a professor at N. C. State University and the photographer was Jack F. Dermid with the North Carolina Wildlife Resources Commission, both in Raleigh, N.C.

The professor was studying wood duck nesting activities by placing nesting boxes in nearby areas, and the photographer was attracted to these studies as a way of gaining insight and photographs of nesting details and telling a conservation story.

*A pair of wood ducks is perched on a log.*

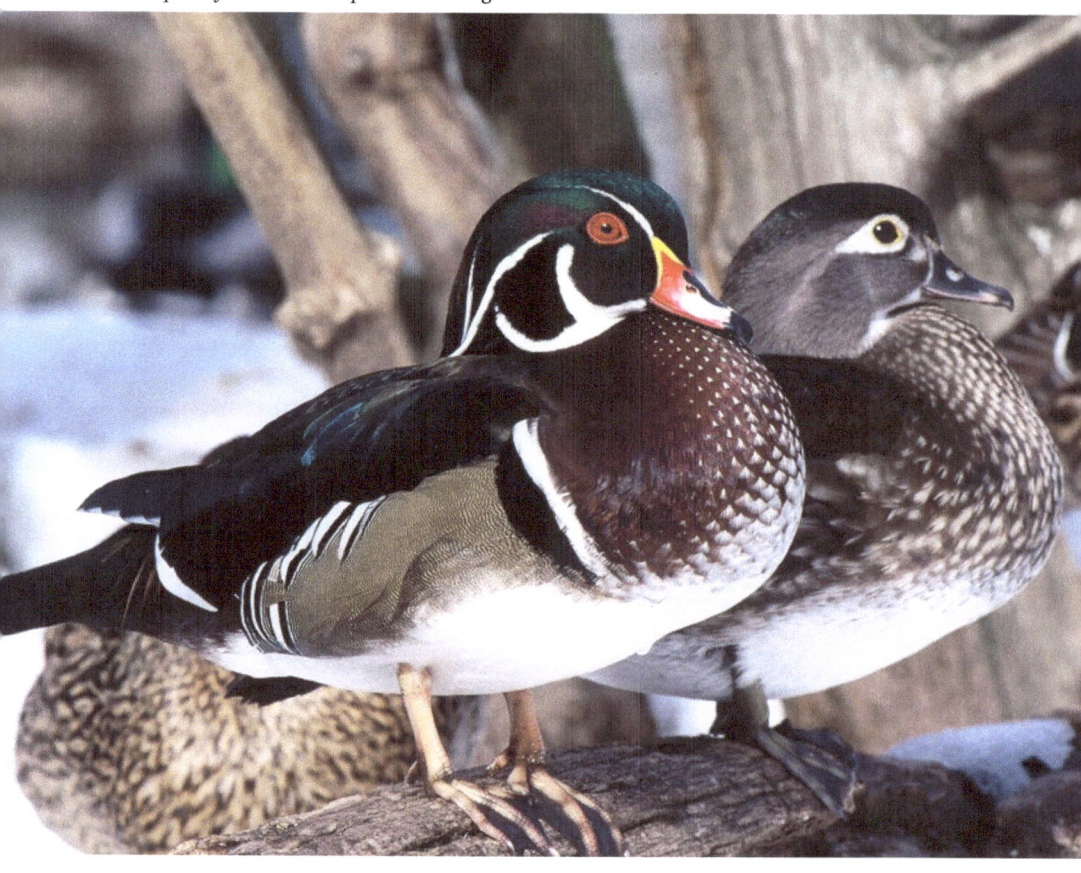

# HOW THE STUDY BEGAN

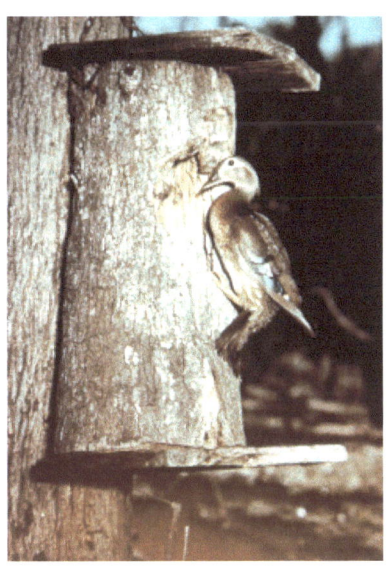

Most ducks make their nests in the prairie pothole region of the northern United States, or in Canada and Alaska where they build their nests in upland vegetation or marshes. But the wood duck is different. It nests in hollow trees! Also, most species of ducks migrate each spring to far northern areas for nesting, but many wood ducks remain in North Carolina and other southeastern states throughout the year.

*Our first nest box was made from a section of a hollow log and hung in a small swamp at Dr. J. R. Hester's pond. (Photo by Jack Dermid)*

When we learned that wood ducks use tree cavities for their nests, we were excited. It awakened an intense interest in us, a desire to provide nesting opportunities, and learn more about this interesting wood duck behavior.

We searched for a hollow tree we could put in a swamp. Finally, we found a hollow log and placed it in a small swamp on a local farm pond. There was already a notch cut in one side of the log that could serve as an entrance. We added a board on the top and bottom, and hung it on the side of a tree in early summer. Soon, a gray squirrel used it for its own nest.

The next year in March as we approached the log to remove the old squirrel nest, we were surprised when a female wood duck flew out. She was already incubating a nest with nine eggs!

This early success inspired us to make nest boxes from any suitable material we could find, including old boards, and even a wooden nail keg. We added a few boxes on that pond, and soon began adding boxes in other areas. We tried to make the boxes as inconspicuous as possible, and placed them deep in swamps. We later realized that we actually hid some of them from the ducks. The more conspicuous ones were much more readily used.

Eventually, with the help of many college students and others we had nearly 200 improved nest boxes made of cypress boards which we placed on eleven nearby areas. We added about four inches of coarse sawdust to each box for the hen to use in making a bowl-shaped nest.

# THE NESTING SEQUENCE

We examined each box at least once a week, and started identifying nest box usage, dates nesting started, numbers of eggs and hatching success.

Sometimes other birds, especially hooded mergansers, great crested flycatchers and screech owls, would nest in the boxes. And occasionally smaller birds would nest in them, too, including prothonotary warblers and bluebirds. Wasps also liked to make their nests there.

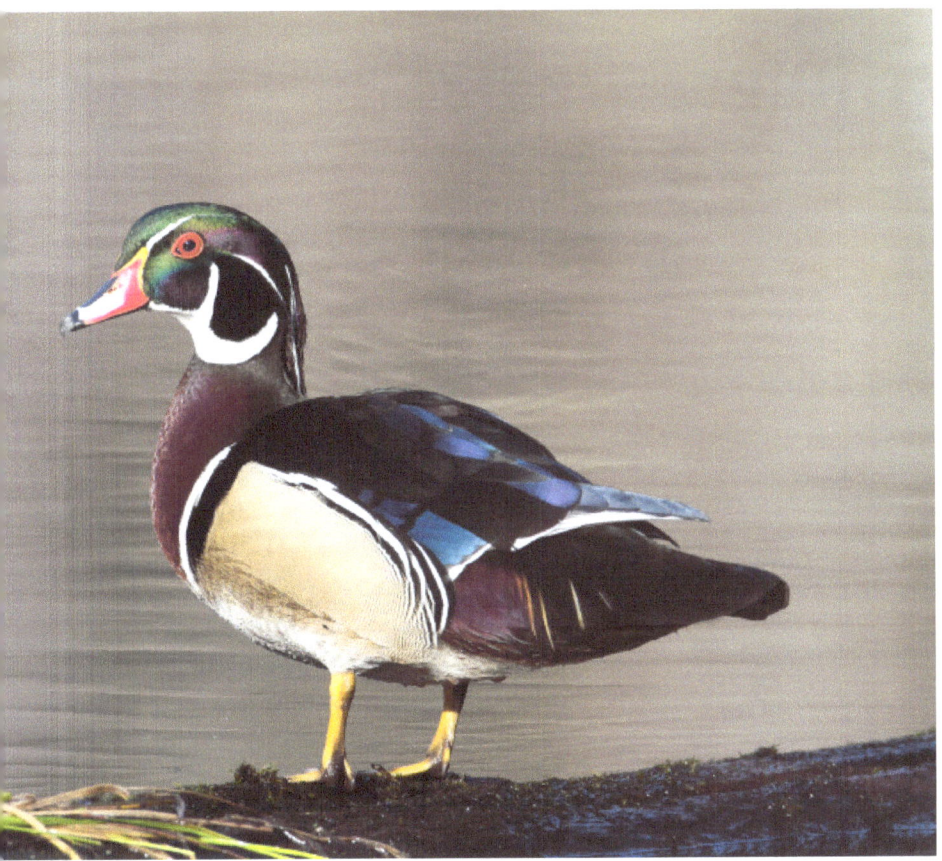

*A drake wood duck waits on a log while the hen is laying an egg in a nearby nest box.*

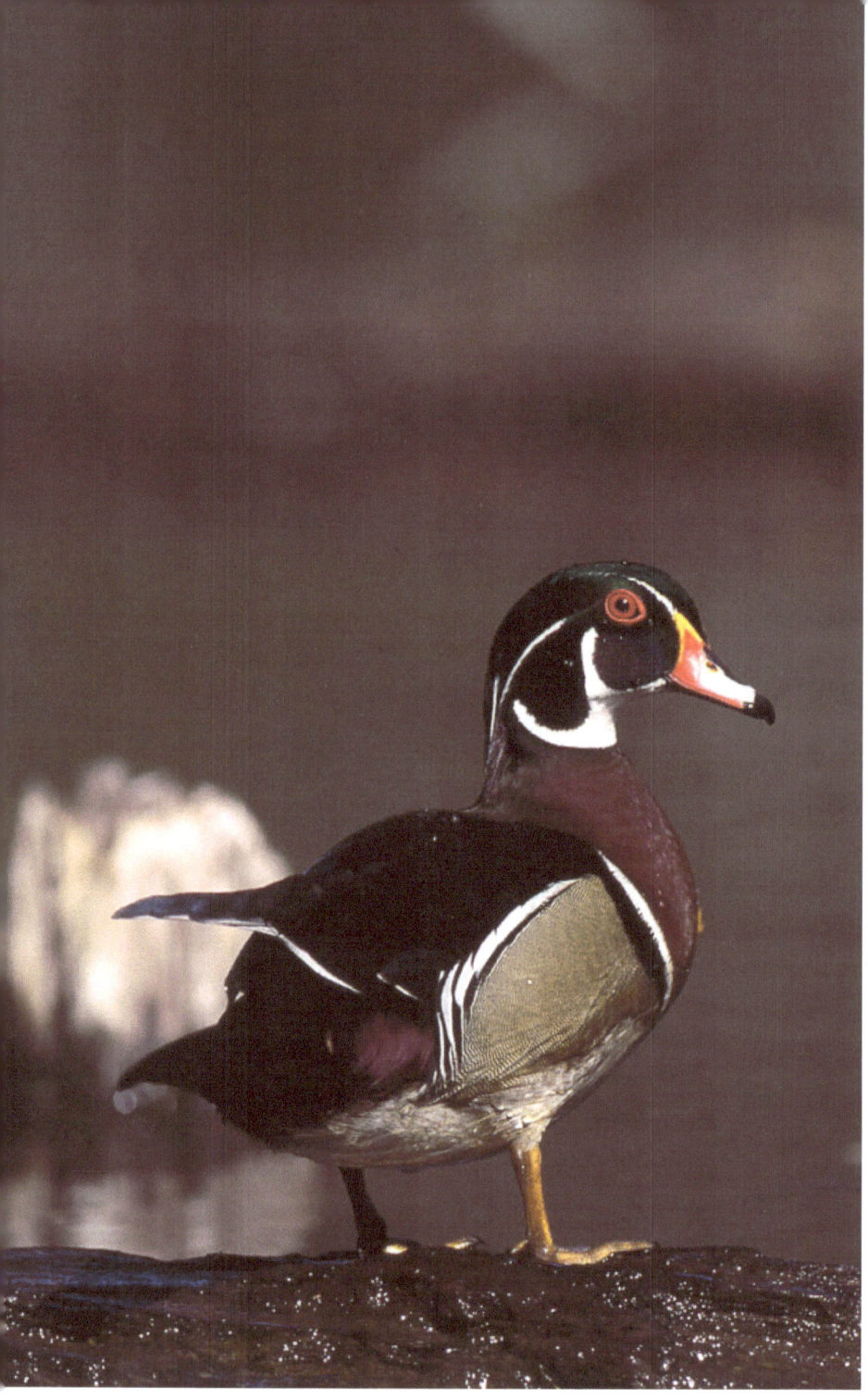

*A beautiful drake wood duck stands on a log in a beaver pond.*

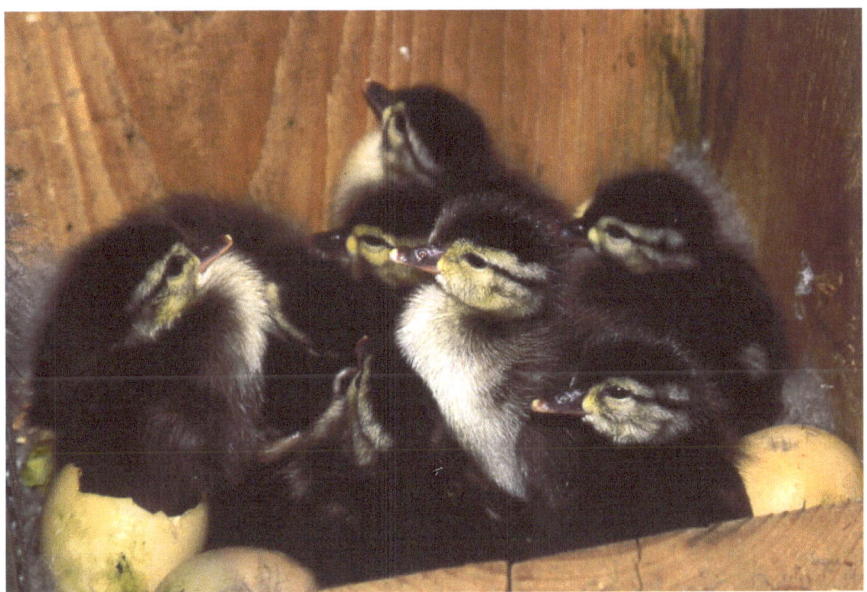

*These day-old ducklings are ready to leave the nest. Notice the white deciduous egg tooth on the end of their bills, used to cut the eggshell open.*

We found that each year nesting began during winter with the earliest nests being started in February. A hen would lay an egg each day and cover the eggs with sawdust when she left. When she had laid about six eggs she would start pulling down feathers from her breast to line the nest. She would continue laying eggs until her clutch was complete with about 12 to 15 eggs, then she would start incubating them. Each time she would leave the nest to feed, she would cover the eggs with the warm down feathers she had previously placed in the nest.

During courtship, the search for a nesting site, and continuing into the early egg-laying period, the drake would always accompany the hen. He would wait on top of the box or nearby on the water or a tree limb while she was in the nest.

But during incubation when the hen was on the nest for long periods of time, the drake would gradually lose interest. From that time on, the hen assumed all responsibilities for the eggs and later the young.

The incubation time for wood duck eggs is about 30 days, but it can vary by several days. At the end of incubation, the egg would

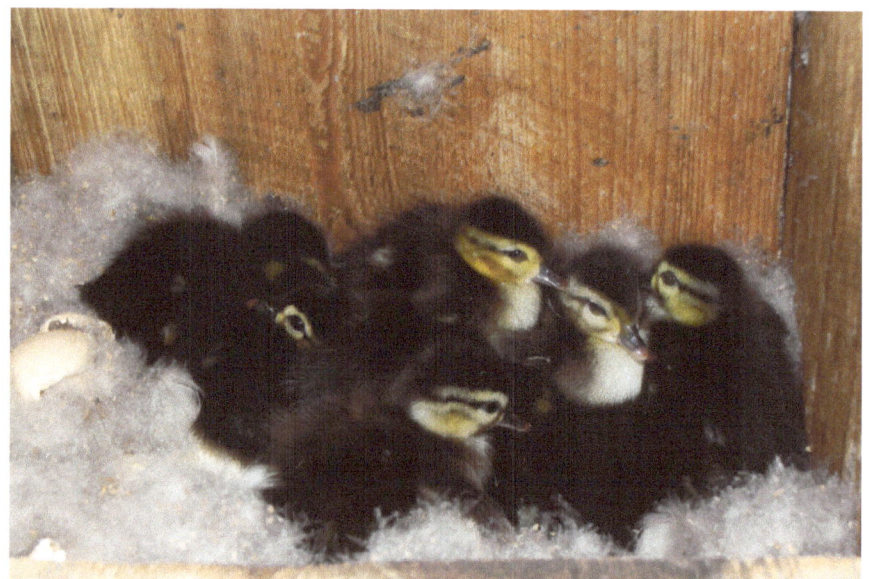

*Now dried off, the day-old ducklings are waiting for their mother to call them from the nest.*

be pipped as the duckling began using its deciduous egg tooth to punch a tiny hole in the shell. By rotating inside the egg and using that egg tooth like a miniature can opener it cuts a circular opening near the large end of the egg.

When the duckling emerges from the egg it is weak and wet, but after spending several hours with its mother, it is dry and fluffy. It soon gains strength and within 24 hours is ready to leave the nest.

# BROOD REARING AREAS

Wood ducks usually choose a nest site in a hollow tree or nest box in a swamp or marsh, but we learned that some hens choose a tree cavity far from water. Many nests have been found in cities, especially in parks or residential areas with large trees with existing cavities. Regardless as to where the nest is located, immediately after the young leave the nest the hen will lead the ducklings to a brood-rearing area in a marsh or swamp, sometimes requiring travel over land for long distances. This exposes them to additional predators along the way, where they are unable to use some of their normal defenses of swimming and diving.

For their first several weeks, young wood ducks feed mainly on insects and other animal matter. Some of the best brood rearing areas are those with thick aquatic vegetation, where the ducklings find a lot of aquatic insects. The thick vegetation also allows them to remain easily hidden.

As is true with all species of ducks and many other species of birds, initial mortality is high. Predators range from bass and pickerel to minks, hawks, owls, snakes and any other predator found in the same habitat. Even bullfrogs have been known to eat them.

Survival varied greatly between the broods we studied, probably reflecting variation in parental guidance and differences in the quality of brood-rearing habitat. We felt that on average, less than half of the ducklings survived to reach flight at about nine or 10 weeks of age.

*A web tag is applied to the foot of a day-old duckling which later provides information on its age and origin.*

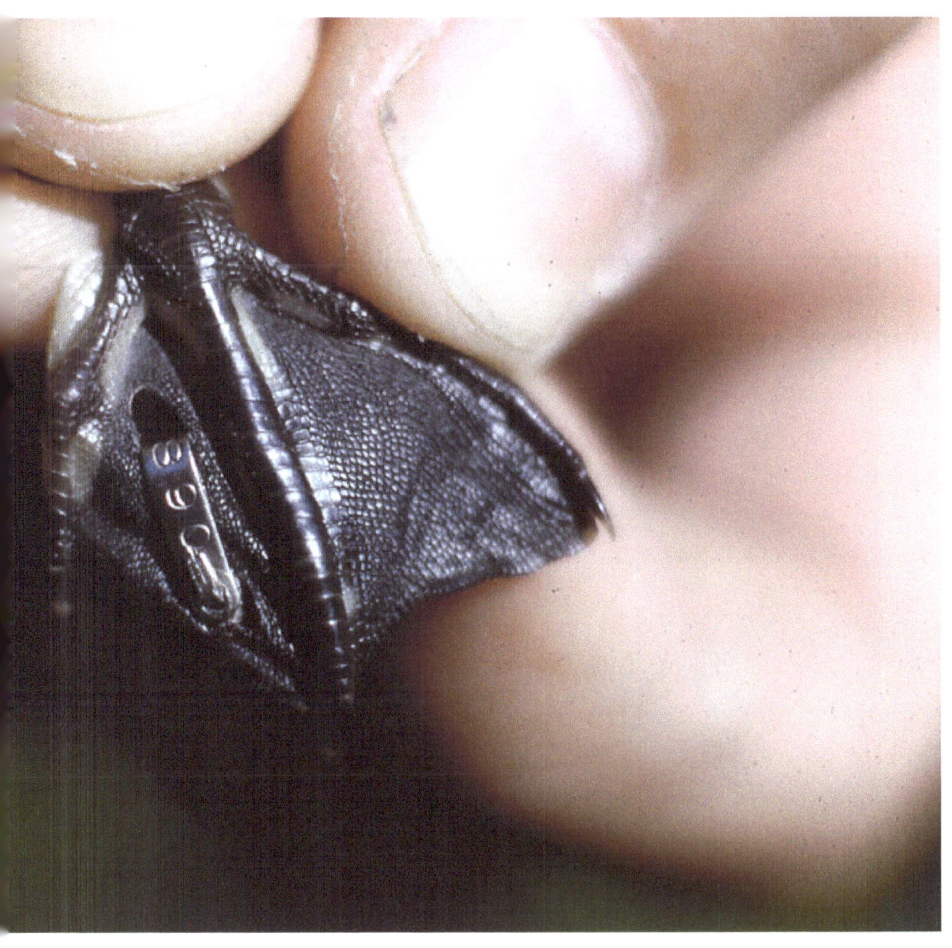

## BANDING AND WEB TAGGING

After studying nesting habits for several years, we began more advanced projects by banding the females while they were incubating their eggs. Catching the hen on the nest was often a challenge because many of them would hear us coming and flush from the nest. But if we succeeded in finding her there, we trapped her inside by placing a hunting sock filled with leaves in the box entrance. Then we would remove her and place a numbered aluminum band on her leg.

We learned a lot about individual ducks from the bands. We were able to tell if an individual hen nested twice in a single year, and if she returned the following year. We also determined whether she returned to the same nest box.

After marking the hens with leg bands our next adventure was to mark the baby ducks by placing tiny numbered metal tags in the webs of their feet when they were only one day old. This was an especially challenging project because the baby ducks are only in the nest for one day after hatching. We had to intensify our observation of the eggs to predict when they would hatch. We learned that as hatching time approached; if we held an egg to our ear we could hear a faint pecking sound made by the baby duck as it began pecking its way out of the egg.

As hatching time approached there would be a sequence of first hearing the ducklings pecking inside the egg, next the eggs being pipped, then hatched young still wet and finally, fluffy ducklings ready to leave the nest.

Often these steps followed at about one day intervals, but we found the time for them varied widely. In some nests, for example, the eggs might remain pipped for two or three days, and then within 24 hours they would hatch and all leave the nest. The ducklings talk to each other and to their mother while they are still in the egg, and this apparently helps synchronize the hatching and bonding processes.

Determining when the baby ducks would be hatched and ready for tagging was a real challenge. But for most nests, dedicated students succeeded in being there during that brief period to catch them and place the tags.

When properly applied, the tags remained throughout the life of the duck and revealed its exact age and place of origin.

We also banded ducklings in brood rearing areas in marshes

and swamps when they were several weeks old by catching them in traps baited with corn. If they had web tags we could determine their age and how far they had traveled. We could also measure their growth and determine the age at which they began to fly.

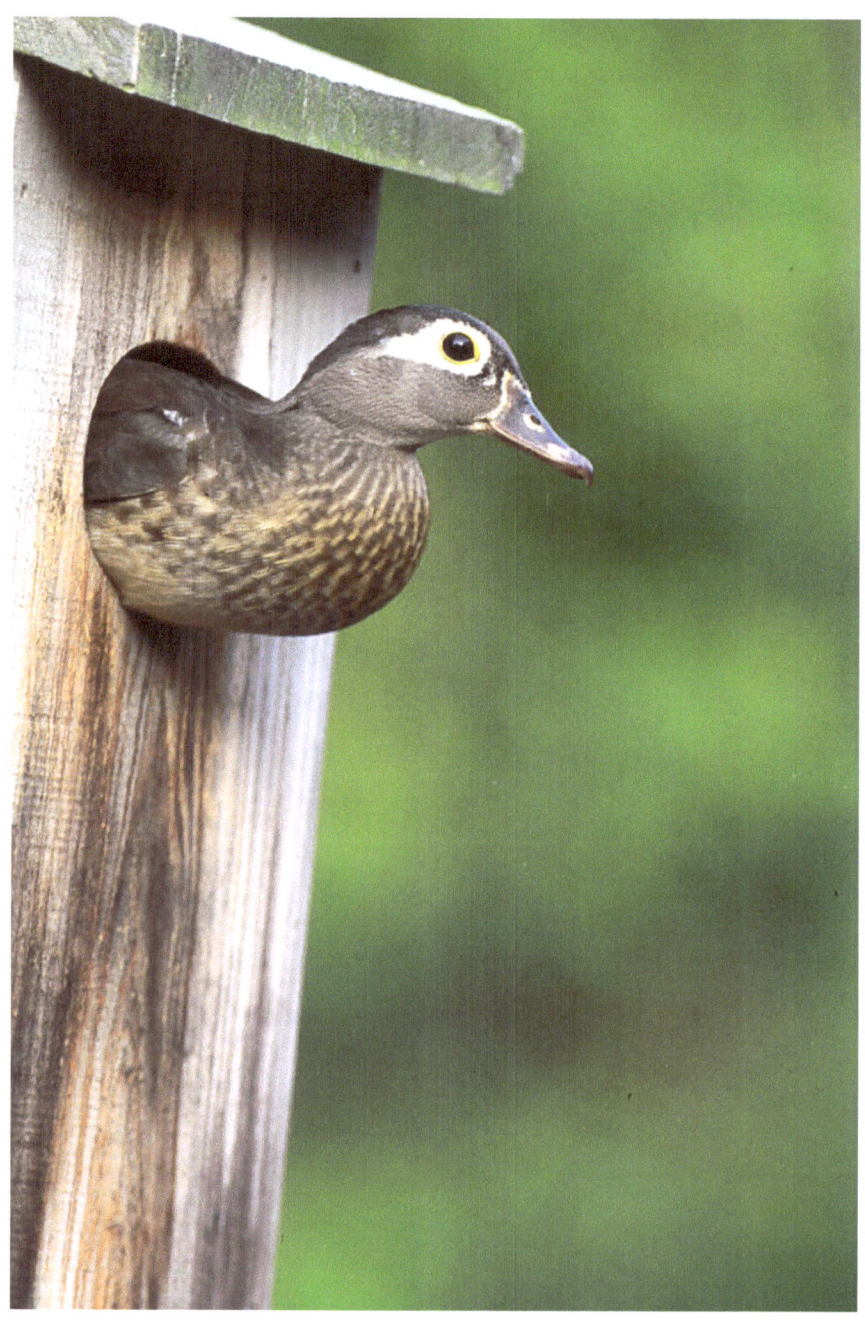

*A hen wood duck looks cautiously from the nest making sure it is safe to call her ducklings.*

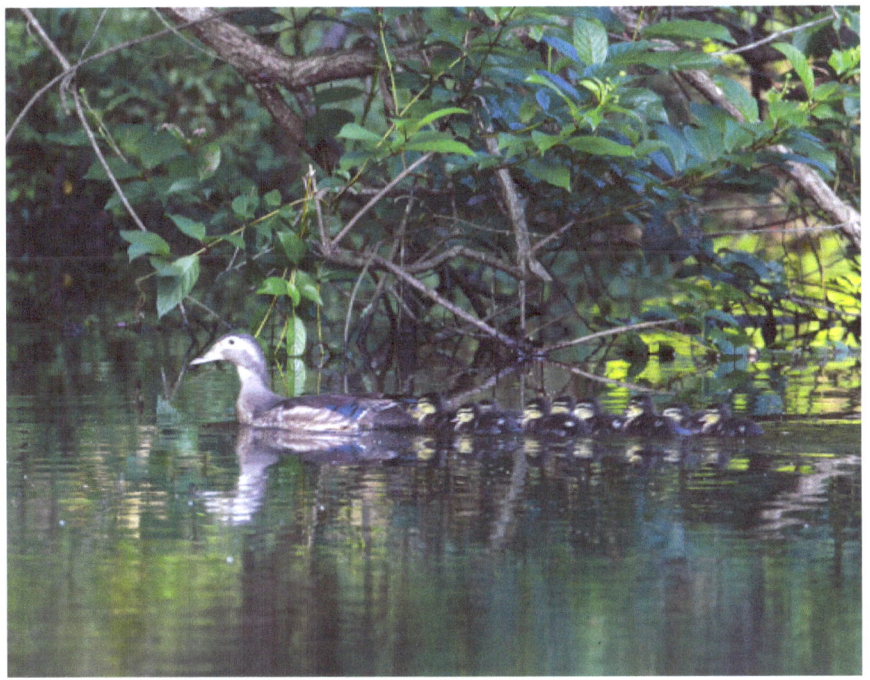

*A wood duck hen leads her newly hatched young to the safety of dense aquatic vegetation.*

# PHOTOGRAPHING
# NESTING DUCKS

Having detailed records of each nest provided valuable insight into when each nest would be hatching, and which nests would be the best ones for Jack's photography. For a photographer wanting to photograph the ducklings leaving the nest, this was essential information. We placed photography blinds near the best nests, and each time we checked the nests, we moved the blinds closer. By hatching time, each blind was near the nest and the hen had become accustomed to it.

Jack found that it was often necessary to wait patiently in the blind for several hours while the hen made her decision to leave the nest and call her young to jump out.

Usually the exodus was in early to mid-morning, but on one occasion, Jack had to wait from 7 a.m. until 4 p.m. for the hen to call the ducklings from the box.

Jack always checked the box on the morning of the exodus to assure that the ducklings were there and ready to leave, otherwise he might be left waiting and watching an empty box after they had already left. Also there was the possibility that the ducklings were not sufficiently dry

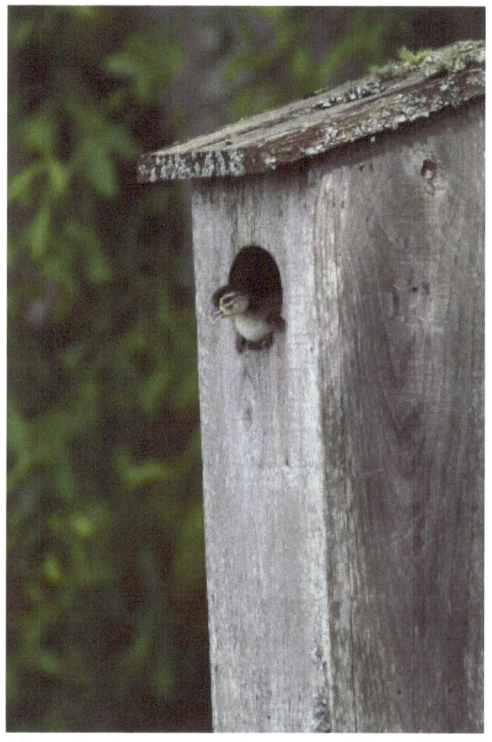

*The exodus from most wood duck nests happens rapidly, and sometimes two ducklings jump together.*

and therefore not ready to leave that day.

We found that when we checked on young ducks that were dry and ready to leave the nest, it was important to do so quietly. A loud noise or bumping the box could excite the ducklings and cause them to spontaneously start jumping from the box in the absence of the mother.

We wanted to know more about how the ducklings actually climb out of the cavity. We found no references in the literature that satisfied our curiosity, so we built a nest box with a glass back and placed it in the front of a boathouse to find out. A hinged door covered the glass back of the nest box except when we were making observations.

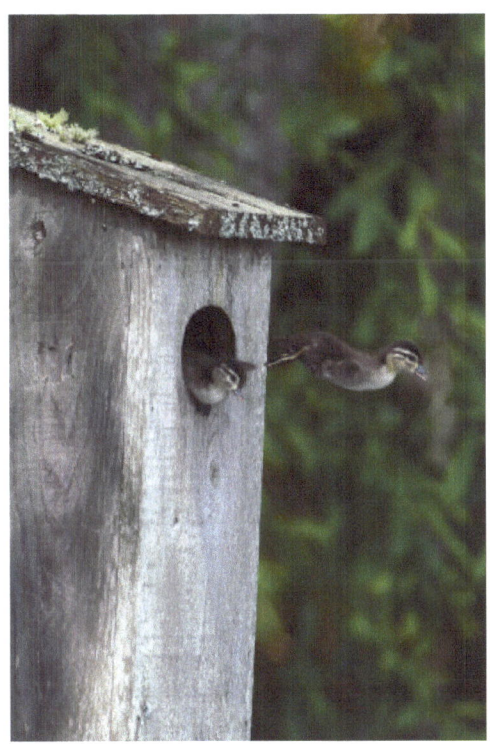

*Responding to their mother's call, these baby wood ducks leap fearlessly from the nest.*

It was relatively dark inside the boathouse, and we made our observations from a burlap blind behind the box. Fortunately our gamble that a wood duck would nest in the box paid dividends.

On the morning of the exodus, Jack uncovered the glass and slipped into the blind while the hen was away from the nest. The hen was somewhat conditioned to having the door open, for we had observed and photographed activities in the nest the previous evening. When she returned, she seemed in no way inhibited by the exposed condition of her nest. She appeared in the entrance and without hesitation dropped down over the young to brood them.

When the time came for the exodus, the hen perched in the entrance of the box for a while before dropping to the water and begin calling.

Her calls triggered a response in the young almost immediately, and they began jumping up and down in the direction of the nest entrance. Jack compared the jumping to popping popcorn, except that it was directional. The nest was filled with a frenzy of activity and the answering calls of the ducklings.

One thing was certain, the ducklings did not climb out as we

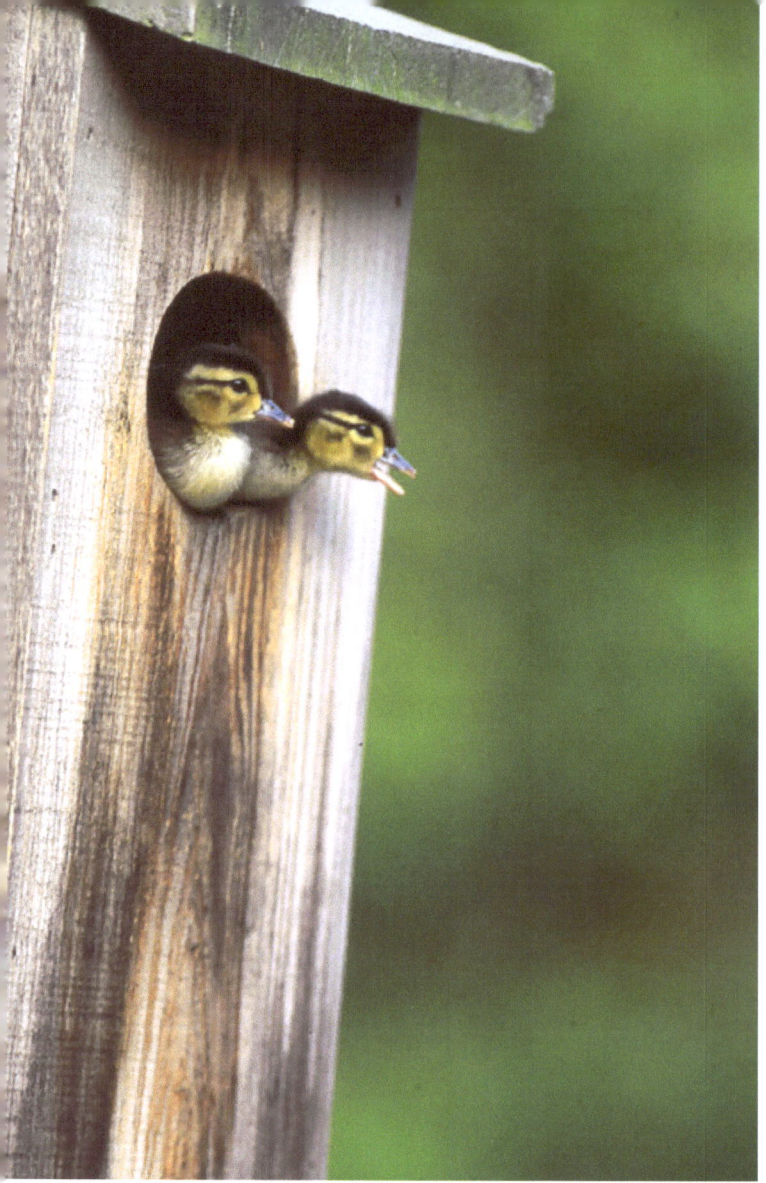

*A wood duck hen patiently waits near her nest box to assure that all of her young have left.*

had expected. Instead, they jumped toward the entrance repeatedly. When one of them hit against the front panel of the box in the right way, its sharp claws caught in the rough wood, anchoring it in position. The duckling rested a moment, then lurched straight upward to gain another claw hold. A series of three or more successful hitches were usually required to reach the entrance 16 inches above the nest.

Quite a bit of chance was involved in securing a claw hold and in making each successive hitch upward. Sometimes a duckling would almost reach the top only to fall back. At other times, a duckling would be knocked from its position by another youngster. Sometimes two or more would collide in midair. But as the numbers in the nest thinned, those remaining had an easier time.

Finally, the nest was empty and all was quiet. Jack looked through the entrance hole in the box to see the hen swimming toward the distant shore with her family tightly clustered behind her.

Jack filmed a dramatic movie of the events inside the box, including the exodus. The movie became a highlight of the film Wildlife Babies that Jack produced for the N.C. Wildlife Resources Commission. It was voted as the best wildlife movie of the year by the Outdoor Writers Association of America.

Undoubtedly, the call of the hen from outside the nest induces the young to leave. We then went to another nest box to photograph the day-old ducklings while the hen was away. The box was on a post on an island, and to simplify photography we placed it on the ground. When the top was removed, we found the ducklings huddled in a mass, even their heads were buried. We stirred the young gently with our hands in an effort to get some of them to look up for a more interesting picture, but all they wanted to do was huddle together.

After a while, we placed youngster after youngster in the entrance to the nest, facing outward to see if it would jump. To our amazement, none did. All of them turned back to join their nest mates.

Then suddenly, to our surprise, the hen began calling to the ducklings from a hiding place nearby. We did not see her, but the ducklings heard her and responded. The huddled mass became very much alive and the ducklings began hitching up the inside of the nest box. Moments earlier we could not coax them to leave the nest; now we could not keep them in. The only thing to do was make a hasty retreat so the anxious hen could gather her family together. She was successful and they quickly swam out of sight into thick vegetation.

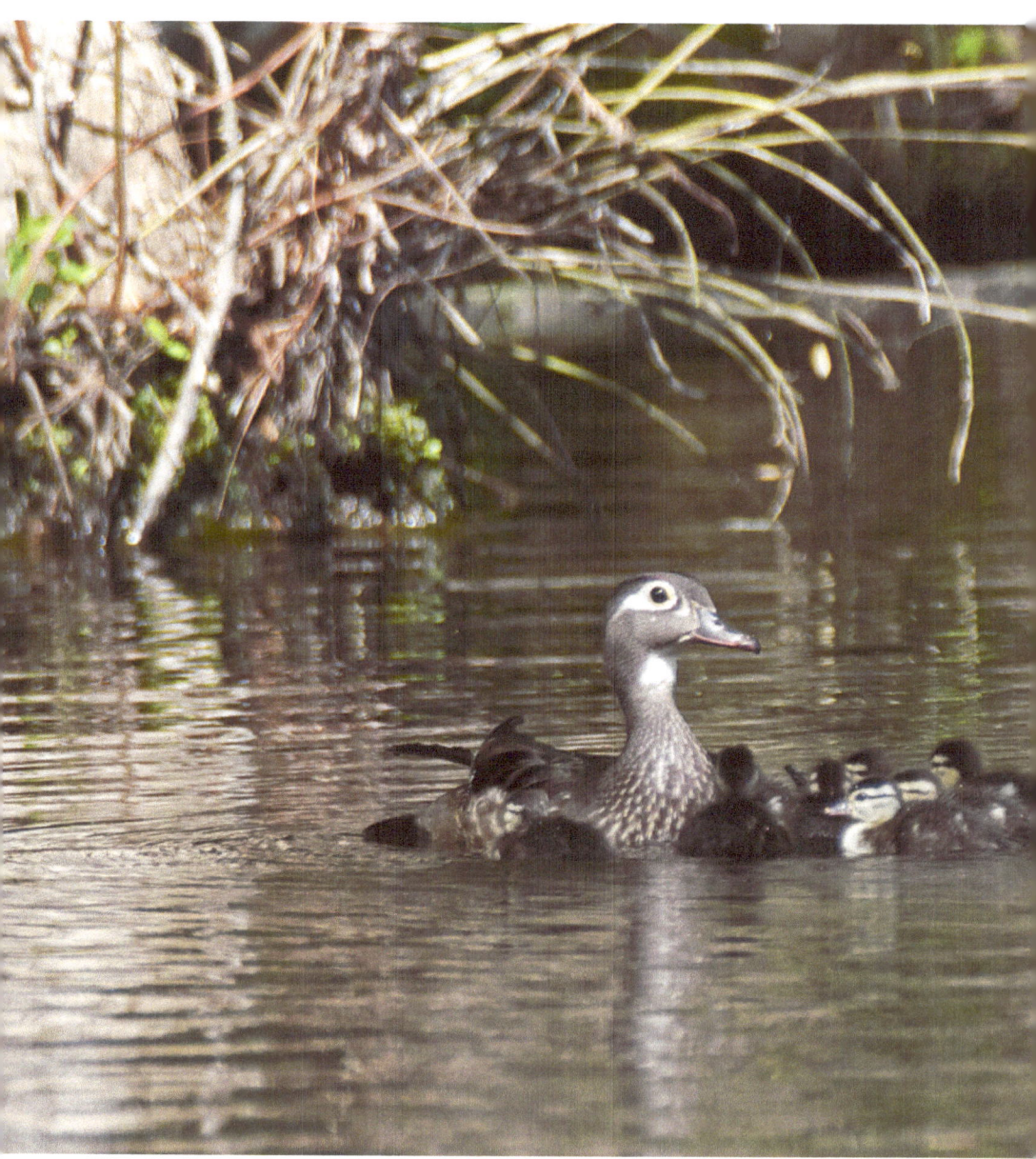

*This wood duck hen waits for all of her ducklings to jump from the nest.*

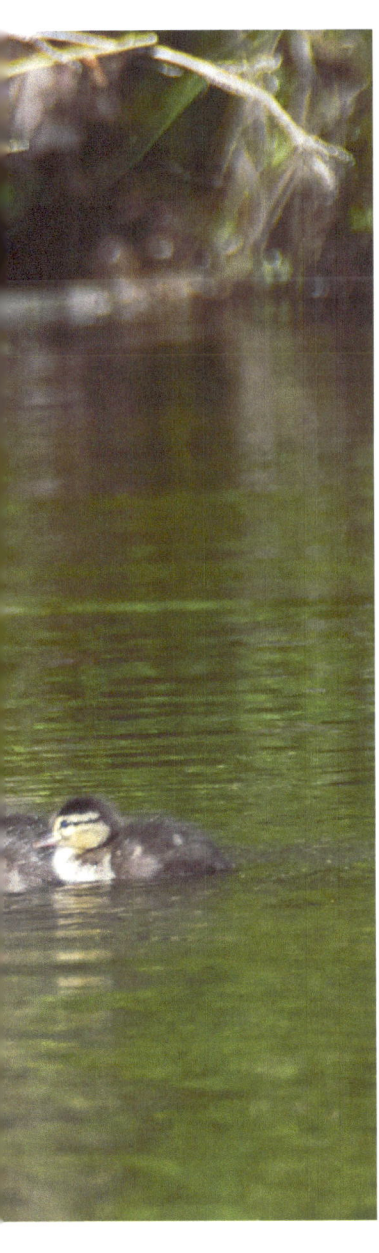

# PHOTOGRAPHING DUCKS IN SWAMPS

We wanted to photograph the ducklings as they were growing up, so we placed photography blinds in several brood rearing areas in nearby millponds and beaver swamps. Our blinds were made of plywood or canvas. Some of them were placed on posts driven into the mud, while others were placed on shore. We situated them where the morning sun would provide good light, and placed corn for food in shallow water or on floating boards near the blinds.

We would enter the blind in early morning, often even before daylight to minimize disturbance of the ducks. Sometimes we waited for long periods for the ducks to arrive. At times they would stay nearby in thick vegetation, hesitant to expose themselves. On some days it became a long waiting game; we were waiting for them to come to us, but they seemed to be waiting for us to leave. Usually the wait paid off and we were able to get our photographs.

*This drake
wood duck
swims
on water
so calm
that he
provides
a perfect
reflection.*

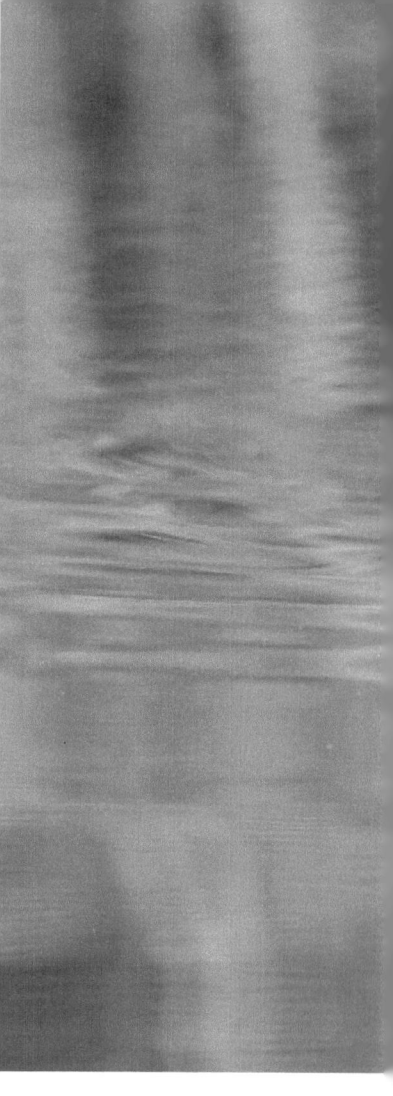

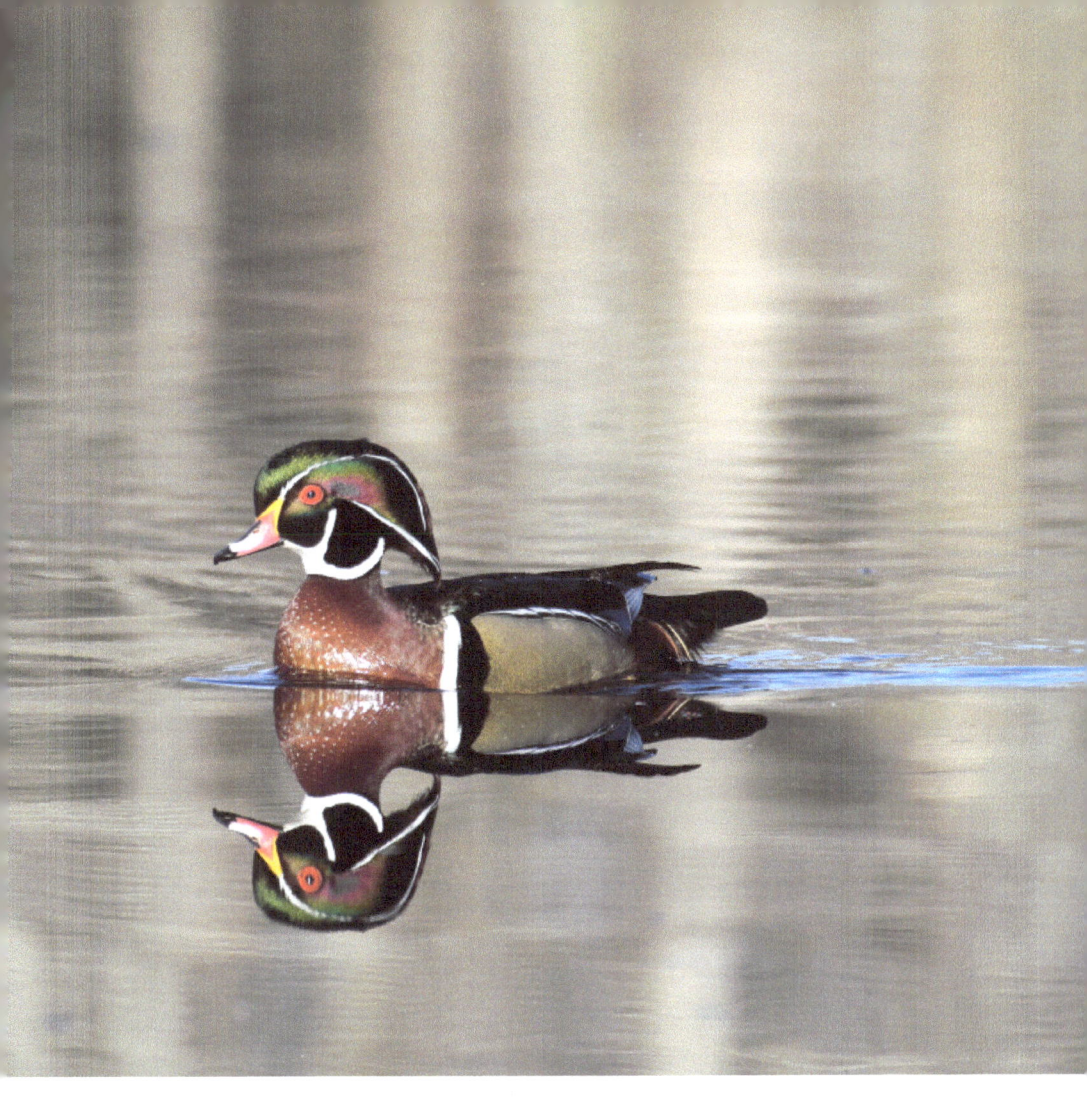

## OTHER EXCITING FINDINGS

From our many observations we learned interesting and exciting things about wood ducks. The banding and web-tagging gave us insight into the lives of individual ducks, and told us things we could never have known otherwise.

From the banding information we learned that hens usually returned to the same pond and even to the same nest each year. When a hen found a nest site that was safe, she would continue to use it year after year. But if the nest was destroyed, she would find

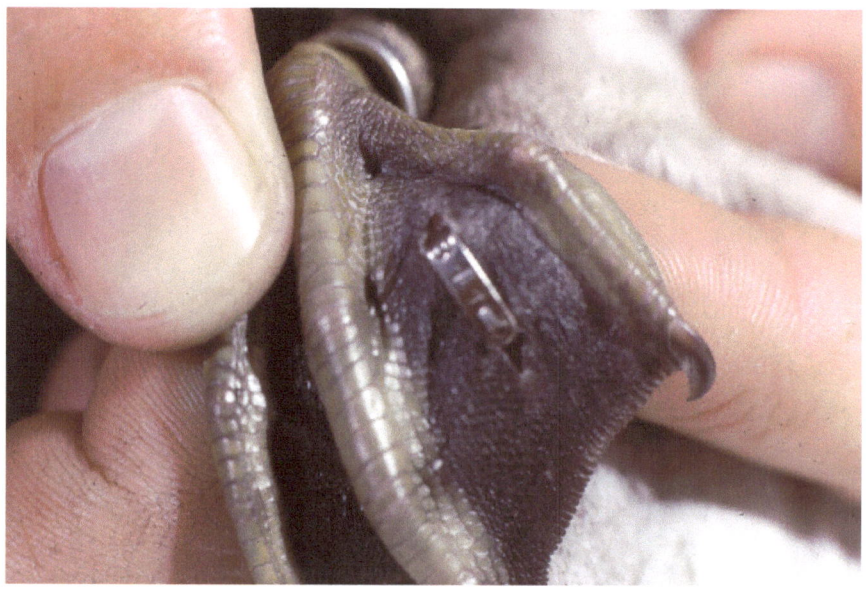

*An adult wood duck's foot holds both a web tag, applied when it was a day old, and a leg band, affixed when it was older.*

another site for her next nesting attempt.

Not all nests were successful. Raccoons and black rat snakes often destroyed the nests and sometimes would also kill the hens. We found that by placing the box on a post and adding a metal cone as a predator guard under it, we could prevent these predators from reaching the nest. Only snakes longer than six feet could bypass the predator guard. Woodpeckers and perhaps other birds also destroyed some nests by pecking holes in the eggs. Dump nests containing eggs of several hens were often abandoned.

We were surprised to find that about 10 percent of our hens nested twice in a single year. After her ducklings were several weeks old and able to care for themselves, some hens would nest a second time. We initially thought the hen might have lost her first brood through predation or accident, but we found web tagged ducklings that survived from both broods.

We also found that some boxes were used twice in a season.

And in a few rare instances, three successful nests were produced in one box in a single year. Considering that it takes about 15 days to lay the eggs and 30 days to incubate them, the process for a single nest requires about 45 days. So three successive nests would require a minimum of 135 days, and that is almost the length of the entire nesting season.

The banding and tagging of the ducks was under permits from the state and federal conservation agencies, and we provided records about each band and tag we applied. When the duck was killed by a hunter or found in some other way, we were informed about the location of the band or tag recoveries.

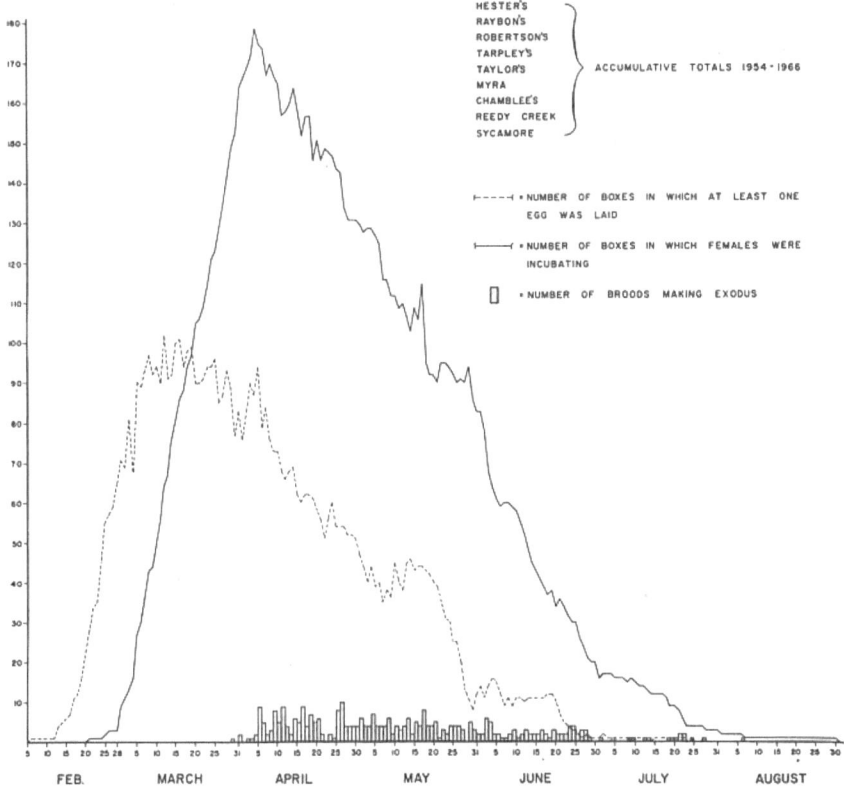

*This graph depicts egg-laying, incubation and exodus from nest boxes for nine study areas over several years.*

# WOOD DUCK MIGRATIONS
# AND BAND RETURNS

Wood ducks roost on the water in swamps, and on many afternoons we waited around sunset near flight lines to count ducks coming to these roosts. From late-September until mid-October the numbers would increase each night reflecting an influx of migrating birds. Migration was mostly over by mid- to late- October before the hunting season began, so band returns by hunters after then told us a lot about where the ducks were spending the winter.

We learned that about half of the band returns from hunters were from places within 25 miles of where we had banded the duck, indicating it had not migrated at all. Most of the remaining band returns were from almost straight south of our banding locations just east of Raleigh, NC. Many of them were from southeastern North Carolina and along the Waccamaw River in South Carolina. Some bands were recovered in Georgia and Florida, and even one from Mississippi.

About 60 percent of our banded hens returned to nest the following year. The oldest wood duck hen in our study was nine years old.

Because the tiny web tags only had a number without any other message, we never envisioned that they would be meaningful to anyone other than ourselves. But on several occasions people found the tagged ducklings in various ways and contacted the N.C. Wildlife Resources Commission which had provided us permission for using the tags. Then they contacted us to inquire about it and tell us where they found the duckling.

Wood duck pairs are formed during autumn or on the wintering grounds, after ducks have congregated from different states. Because of this, ducks from widely separated areas are likely to become pairs. One of the most interesting parts of this new relationship is that the hen returns to where she was born and the drake simply follows her there. Hens hatched on our study areas would return there to nest, but they were very likely to have mates that had hatched in another area, often in another state.

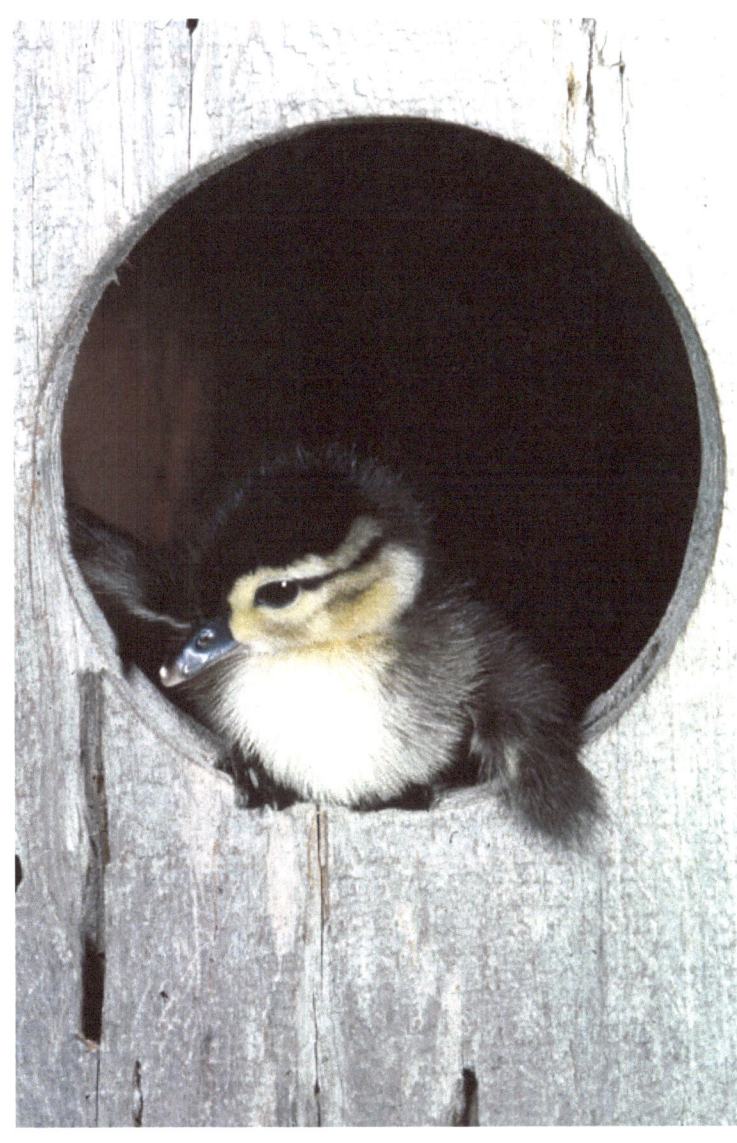

*Day-old duckling gets its first look at the outside world, preparing to jump to the water. (Photo by Jack Dermid)*

# UNUSUAL WOOD DUCK BEHAVIOR

Wood ducks do many things that seen illogical to humans. Nesting so far from aquatic brood rearing areas certainly seems to be one of them, and the overland trek with its additional exposure to predators and accidents probably reduces brood survival.

One of our most successful areas was Dr. J. R. Hester's pond about 20 miles east of Raleigh, N.C. It was on a tributary of Little River. Tarpley's Millpond was about two miles upstream on that river, and was both a good nesting location and brood rearing area. After we began web tagging ducklings, we found ducklings that had been lead there from Hester's pond as well as those hatched there on Tarpley's Millpond.

Some hens will lead their ducklings to distant brood rearing areas, when what appears to be equally good habitat is nearer. In one case, a man found a hen and her brood crossing a road and contacted us with the web tag numbers and location. We determined that the ducklings had hatched on Hester's pond the previous day. They had been led across Little River and were apparently headed over land to a swamp in the Buffalo Creek watershed. In this case, the hen was leading her brood overland for four miles across a river in one watershed to a swamp in a different watershed. Traps placed in that swamp confirmed other web tagged ducklings were also in that swamp when they were too young to have flown there. Some of the web-tagged ducklings there were only 23 days old, much too young to fly.

Nesting irregularities apparently are more frequent in areas with heavy nesting density. One of the most obvious is the simultaneous utilization of a single nest box by several females, in which they each lay eggs, sometimes accumulating dozens of them. This is called dump nesting, and seems to reflect a social nature of this species and perhaps confusion about initiating individual nests.

This happens most often early in the nesting season, and many of these nests are abandoned by all of the hens. Dump nesting seems especially strange since another equally good nest box

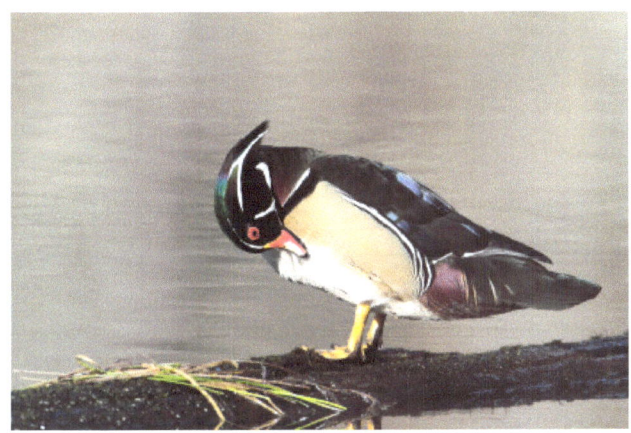

*This wood duck drake preens himself to maintain his beautiful plumage.*

might remain unused nearby.

But sometimes one hen will claim the nest and incubate her eggs along with those of other hens, for a total of 20 or more eggs. Our largest successful dump nest contained 36 eggs, 30 of which hatched.

When we were web-tagging the ducklings in the nest, the typical process was to approach the nest box and open it. Usually this would cause the hen to flush from the nest.

Then we would remove the ducklings and place them in a tall bucket. After applying the tag to the web of the foot of each duckling, they would be returned to the nest and allowed to settle down and wait for the return of the hen.

Individual ducks have personalities just as humans do. Some of them are more tolerant of human disturbance than others. In one case when we opened the box, the hen did not leave even when we reached into it. She remained, and we were able to reach under her and remove each duckling while feeling around her legs. After applying the tags, we returned the ducklings to their mother and left the area. She accepted this and never flushed from the nest.

# POPULATION NUMBERS

During the early part of the twentieth century, wood duck populations declined to very low levels. The cause was probably twofold.

First, extensive logging of swamps and river bottom areas destroyed the trees that provided the acorns, beechnuts and other tree seeds that were their primary food. Removing the trees also reduced tree cavities that they needed for nesting.

And secondly, the hunting season at that time extended well into spring. Although most waterfowl species had migrated to relatively remote northern areas by early March, the wood ducks remained in the more heavily populated southern and eastern states where they could be hunted even during their nesting season.

Through the Migratory Bird Treaty and the following Migratory Bird Treaty Act, the hunting season for wood ducks was closed in 1918, and remained closed until 1941 when a bag limit of one bird per day was permitted. Over time the bag limit has been raised as the population further recovered.

The recovery of wood duck numbers was facilitated by restricting the hunting season and by the erection of numerous nesting boxes in suitable habitat throughout their range. Nest box projects became a favorite activity of conservation organizations.

In the early part of the last century beavers had been largely extirpated in most of the eastern United States, resulting in few beavers throughout most of the wood duck's range. As the beaver population numbers increased through restocking and natural range expansion, beavers built dams that provided shallow water in woodland areas. These wetlands provided almost ideal habitat for wood ducks. We have often said that the beaver is the best friend the wood duck ever had.

# ROOSTING

Wood ducks congregate in swamps at sunset and remain on the water there until daybreak. By sunrise, most of them have left and dispersed to feeding areas along wooded streams where they search for acorns and other favorite foods.

One of our earliest adventures with wood ducks was counting them coming to roost in swamps. Some of the areas were only about an acre in size, but others were much larger. Beaver ponds and the swamps at the head of millponds were some of the most frequently used areas.

We noticed that the number of ducks coming to these swamps increased during the month of October, indicating additional birds migrating from more northern areas. And we also noticed that as the month progressed, greater percentages of the ducks came as pairs or multiples of pairs, indicating the beginning of pair formation.

# HUNTING

In modern times wood ducks are hunted by two basic methods. And in most years in North Carolina and in some other southeastern states, the wood duck is the most frequently killed duck.

One favorite hunting technique is to float small creeks and rivers in canoes or john boats and shoot them as they flush. We have had memorable hunts this way. We would select a river section without too many fallen trees or other obstructions blocking passage on the river. Then after finding a section that could be floated in a day, we would float the stream between two road bridges, taking turns at paddling and hunting.

Another method is to hunt them as they enter or leave  roosting swamps.

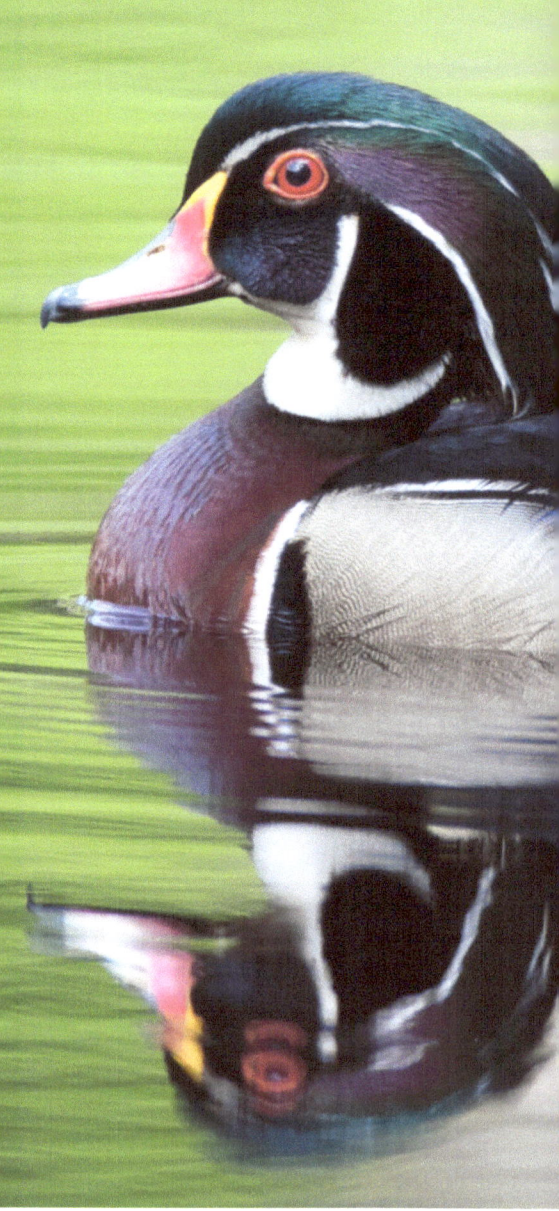

# AUTHOR'S THOUGHTS

Learning of the unique habits and needs of wood ducks and providing them safe nesting sites have been valuable and rewarding projects. Through our observations, photography, and marking techniques, we gained great insight into details of this interesting and beautiful bird that we otherwise would never have known. The conservation benefits of this work have been important, and the unique partnership and friendship that persisted through all of it have been personally rewarding.

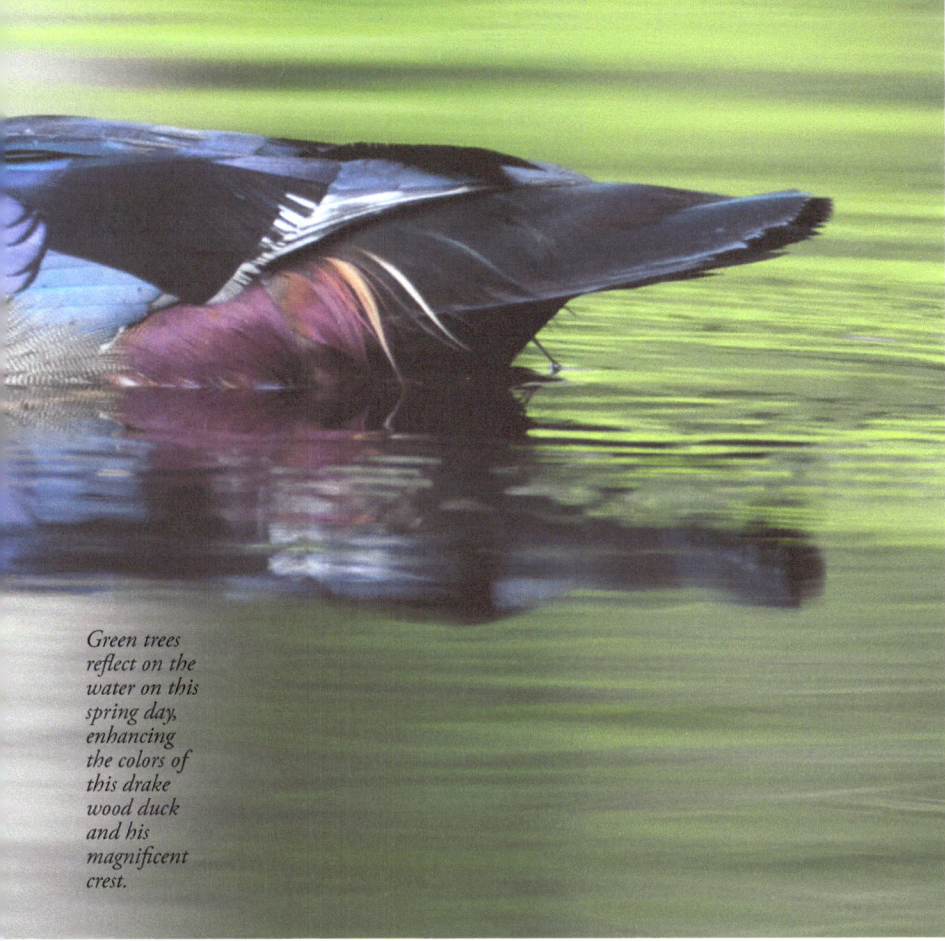

*Green trees reflect on the water on this spring day, enhancing the colors of this drake wood duck and his magnificent crest.*

# ACKNOWLEDGEMENT

Sincere appreciation is extended to Jack Dermid and to all the students, landowners, agencies and others who cooperated in these studies.

Several people facilitated this publication by editing and formatting the text and photographs and otherwise preparing it for publication. My appreciation goes especially to Donnalouise C. Hester, Hugh Cashion and Kevin Rhoades who were most helpful.

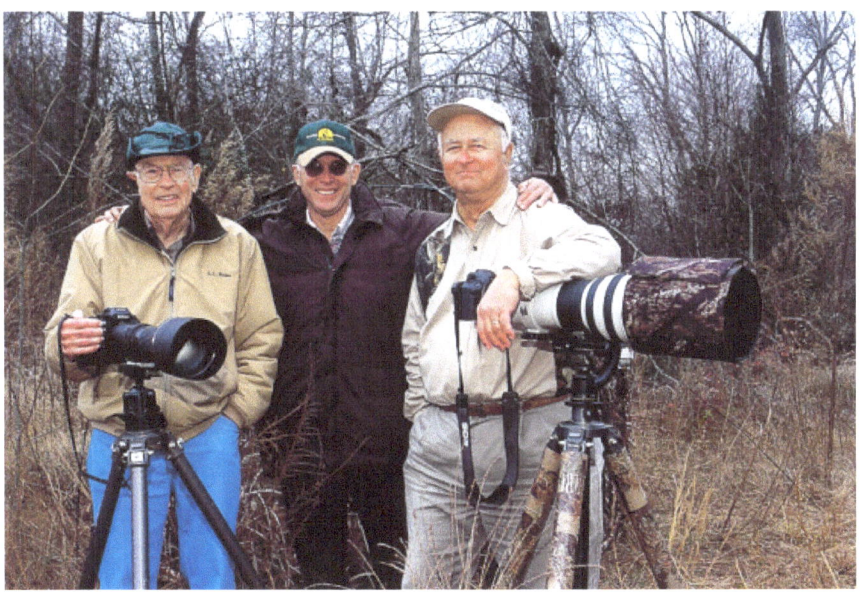

*The author F. Eugene Hester (right) is pictured in the wild with collaborators and assistants Jack F. Dermid (left) and Garland Pardue. (NCWRC photo by Melissa McGaw)*